WHEN WE WENT TO THE
ZOO

Jan Ormerod

Lothrop, Lee & Shepard Books
New York

Ibex

Gibbons

Llama Rides

Pelicans

Elephants

Otters

Orangutans

Penguins

Sea Lions

Toucans

Emus

Sharks

Tropical Fish

Boa Constrictors

Goats

Rabbits

Lions

Camel Rides

Giraffes

Grizzly Bears

When we went to the zoo, we saw

a gibbon swing across Gibbon Island.

The pelican yawned

as we rode past.

We sang, "Hi-de-hi-de-ho,

the elephant is so slow."

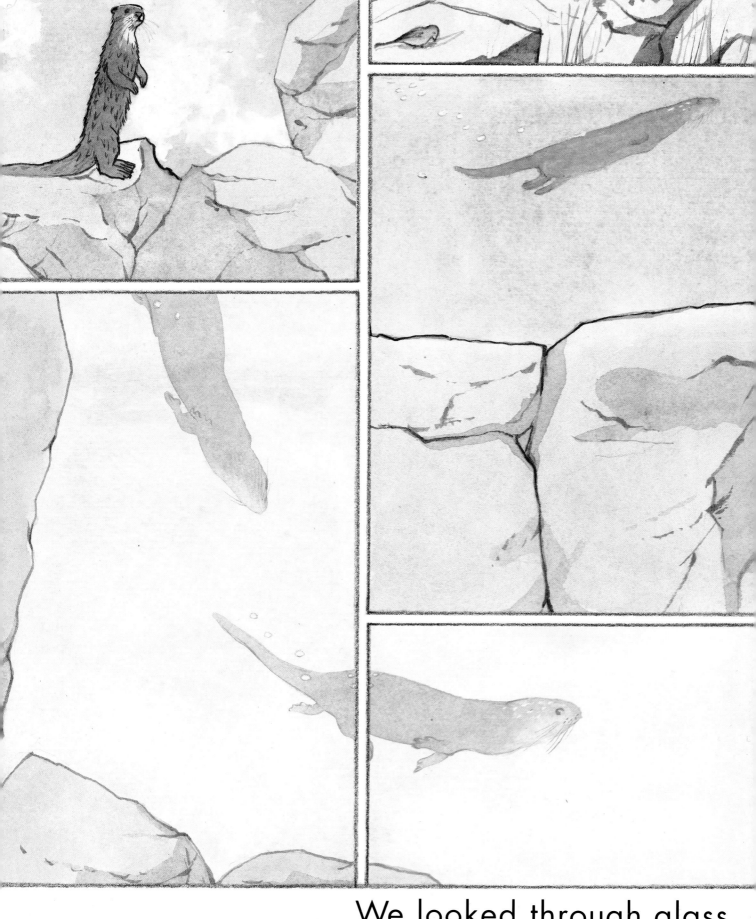

We looked through glass

and saw an otter underwater.

We saw an orangutan carrying a

baby; another had a paper bag.

A penguin playing with a leaf

dived in and out of the water.

We watched the sea lions being fed.

We saw two big-beaked toucans

and some stripy emu chicks.

We saw a shark swimming in the dark,

and fish from a coral reef.

We touched a boa constrictor, a goat,

and a rabbit, which was very soft.

We spent ages looking at a

lion, a lioness, and their cubs.

We sang, "Bumpety, bumpety,

bump, we're on a camel's hump."

giraffe house.

Just past the grizzly bear,

we spied the sparrows.

And in the end we liked

that best, spying the sparrows and their nest.

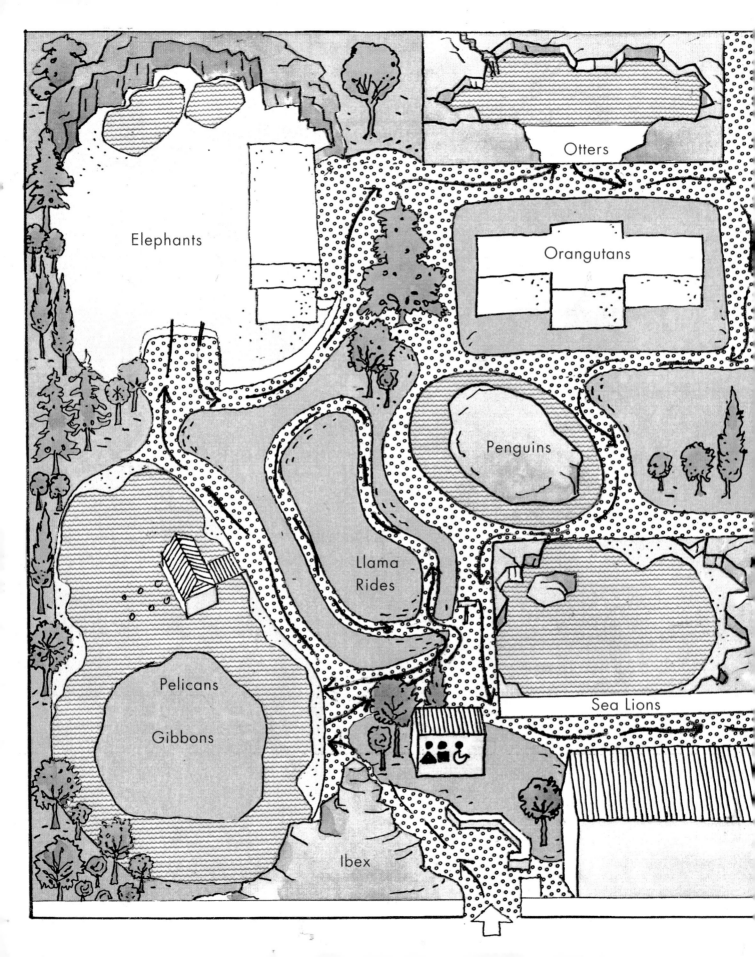

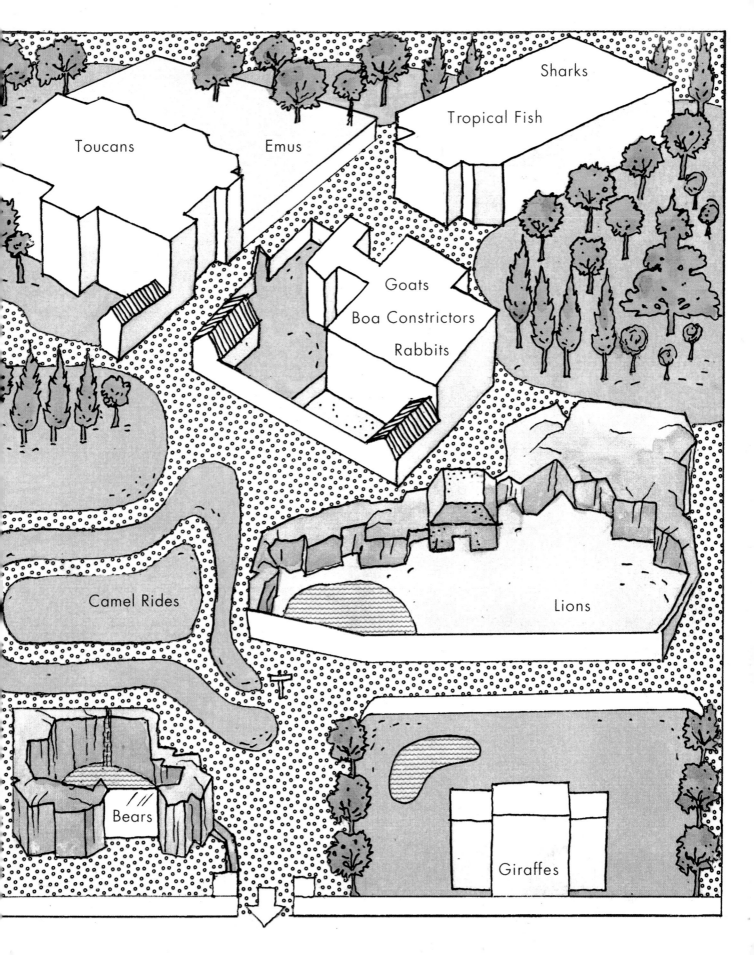

In loving memory of
Peter Bartlett

Copyright © 1990 by Jan Ormerod
First published in Great Britain by Walker Books Ltd.
All rights reserved. No part of this book may be reproduced or utilized in any form or by any
means, electronic or mechanical, including photocopying, recording or by any information
storage and retrieval system, without permission in writing from the Publisher. Inquiries should
be addressed to Lothrop, Lee & Shepard Books, a division of William Morrow & Company, Inc.,
105 Madison Avenue, New York, New York 10016.

Printed in Hong Kong.

First U.S. edition 1991   1 2 3 4 5 6 7 8 9 10

Library of Congress Cataloging in Publication Data
Ormerod, Jan. When we went to the zoo / Jan Ormerod.
p.   cm. Summary: Touring the zoo, two children pet, ride, and observe a variety of animals.
ISBN 0-688-09878-9. — ISBN 0-688-09879-7 (lib. bdg.)   1. Zoos — Juvenile literature.
2. Zoo animals — Juvenile literature.   [1. Zoos.   2. Zoo animals.]   I. Title.
QL76.076   1991   590′.74′4 — dc20   90-6283 CIP AC